THINGS
WE
FEEL

**SOME OTHER BOOKS
BY VARDELL & WONG**

Things We Do

Things We Eat

*Hop to It:
Poems to Get You Moving*

*Pet Crazy:
A Poetry Friday Power Book*

*The Poetry Friday Anthology
for Celebrations*

The Poetry of Science

THINGS WE FEEL

by
Sylvia Vardell & Janet Wong

Pomelo Books

**100% of the profits from this book
will be donated
to the IBBY Children in Crisis Fund**

IBBY CHILDREN IN CRISIS

The IBBY Children in Crisis Fund provides support for children whose lives have been disrupted through war, civil disorder, or natural disaster. The program gives immediate support and help – and also aims for long-term community impact, aligning with IBBY's goal of giving every child the right to become a reader.

ibby.org/awards-activities/ibby-children-in-crisis-fund
usbby.org/donate.html

Special thanks to Renée M. LaTulippe for her ongoing help in editing Pomelo Books publications.

No part of this publication may be reproduced, or stored in a retrieval system, or transmitted in any form or by any means, electronic, mechanical, photocopying, recording, or otherwise, without written permission of the publisher. For information regarding permission, please contact us:

Pomelo Books
4580 Province Line Road
Princeton, NJ 08540
PomeloBooks.com
info@pomelobooks.com

Text/compilation copyright © 2022 by Pomelo Books. All rights reserved.
Individual poems copyright © 2022 by the individual poets. All rights reserved.
Photos sourced from Canva.com and iStockphoto.com.

Library of Congress Cataloging-in-Publication Data is available.
ISBN 978-1-937057-03-9

Please visit us:
PomeloBooks.com

POEMS BY

Marcie Flinchum Atkins
Carmen T. Bernier-Grand
Willeena Booker
Rose Cappelli
Kelly Conroy
Karen Elise Finch
Douglas Florian
Patricia J. Franz
Katey Howes
Carol-Ann Hoyte
Michelle Kogan
Elizabeth Kuelbs
Marty Lapointe-Malchik

Carmela A. Martino
Juli Mayer
Rochelle Melander
Naomi Shihab Nye
Lisa Varchol Perron
Joyce Schriebman
Anastasia Suen
Pamela Taylor
Linda J. Thomas
Fernanda Valentino
Vicki Wilke
Matthew Winter
Janet Wong

TABLE OF CONTENTS

AMAZED	by Carmela A. Martino	9
BRAVE	by Carol-Ann Hoyte	11
CURIOUS	by Michelle Kogan	13
DETERMINED	by Pamela Taylor	15
EXCITED	by Karen Elise Finch	17
FRUSTRATED	by Carmen T. Bernier-Grand	19
GRATEFUL	by Juli Mayer	21
HAPPY	by Fernanda Valentino	23
INSPIRED	by Douglas Florian	25
JEALOUS	by Patricia J. Franz	27
KOOKY	by Joyce Schriebman	29
LONELY	by Linda J. Thomas	31
MAD	by Matthew Winter	33
NERVOUS	by Rose Cappelli	35
OPTIMISTIC	by Janet Wong	37
PROUD	by Lisa Varchol Perron	39
QUEASY	by Katey Howes	41
RESTLESS	by Elizabeth Kuelbs	43

SCARED	by Rochelle Melander	45
TIRED	by Kelly Conroy	47
UPSET	by Vicki Wilke	49
VICTORIOUS	by Anastasia Suen	51
WORRIED	by Naomi Shihab Nye	53
XENIAL	by Willeena Booker	55
YUCKY	by Marty Lapointe-Malchik	57
ZANY	by Marcie Flinchum Atkins	59
ALPHABET CHOICES	by Janet Wong	61

Resources for Parents and Teachers
- Tips for Readers — 64
- Fun Activities to Try — 66
- Web Resources — 68

About the Poets — 70
Poem Credits — 74
About Vardell & Wong — 76
About Pomelo Books — 77
Other Books by Vardell & Wong — 78

AMAZED

by Carmela A. Martino

Look at those eyes –
open so wide,
gazing at me.

Look at that face –
frozen in place,
as close as can be.

It's quite plain to see –
this girl with the curls
is amazed by *me*!

BRAVE

by Carol-Ann Hoyte

My leg brace is my armor
like that of knights
from long ago.

I am just as bold
and just as brave
as they once were.

CURIOUS

by Michelle Kogan

Ooo, there's something there . . .

Whoa, what's that?

Want a peek
through my magical glass?

Hmm,
a marching miniature world.

I'm curious to discover
what they'll do next . . .

DETERMINED

by Pamela Taylor

I'm on the line,
all ready to run.
I want to do well
and also have fun!

I stare straight ahead.
Ears wait for the call.
My heart beats hard.
I'll give it my all!

Determined and set,
I'll find a good pace.
I hope I don't finish
last in this race!

EXCITED

by Karen Elise Finch

Watching.
Waiting.
Anticipating.

Excited to see chemistry!

Bubbles forming.
Here it goes!
Fizzing fast,
it overflows!

FRUSTRATED

by Carmen T. Bernier-Grand

My brother says I must be six
before I use a computer
so I don't "get frustrated."
I wait, wait, and WAIT!!
I am almost six and he is eight.

He accidentally deletes a long paragraph
and gets frustrated.
"I can help," I say.
When he begins to retype,
I push his hand away
and click on "Undo."
His jaw drops slowly as his paragraph
magically reappears.

GRATEFUL

by Juli Mayer

We came to the shelter to pick out a pet –
an older dog to love.
It's all I've been dreaming of.

I knew you were the one when we arrived.
You jumped on me and licked my chin.
My heart opened up and let you in.

As my family walks out, I feel grateful
that I chose you, but now I see –
you chose me!

HAPPY

by Fernanda Valentino

I wriggle and giggle.
You spin me around.
I love riding piggyback
high off the ground.

I'm happy our friendship
is real and true –
I'm happy I have
a good friend like you.

INSPIRED

by Douglas Florian

Nothing has inspired me
as much as our big maple tree.
The rough tough bark
I like to touch.
The bright green leaves
please me so much.
I love the whirling seeds that fly.
I twirl them back up to the sky.
And in mid-March my parents tap
the maple trunk for maple sap!

JEALOUS

by Patricia J. Franz

"Yours is better!"
"You have more!"
"It's not fair!"
You pout. You roar.

But you don't have to
throw a fit
or be unkind.
Just admit:

You're jealous.

KOOKY

by Joyce Schriebman

Willy nilly. I feel silly.
Happy. Snappy. Glad.
Plucky. Ducky. I feel lucky.
There's no room for sad.

Soar like birds.
Make up words.
Ish kabibble. SHOUT!
Fly your quacky wacky flag.
Let your kooky out!

LONELY

by Linda J. Thomas

Your Mama's away
for five whole days.
You feel lonely and lost
without her.
It's okay to be sad for a while –
just remember
what a love-stuffed hug
she'll be saving up
for you,
when she
comes home.

MAD

by Matthew Winter

I want to roar and rattle
and get ready for battle.
I'm MAD!

No! I don't want to talk.
I want to screech and squawk.
I'm MAD!

Breathe in
and
out.

Count 1, 2, 3 –
just like magic
I'm back to me.

NERVOUS

by Rose Cappelli

My tummy's in a
FLIP

My heart is beating
QUICK

I'm feeling kind of nervous –
SNIP!

That didn't hurt a bit!

OPTIMISTIC

by Janet Wong

I can make it –
kick - kick - kick –
to the deep end of the pool.
I see my teacher
waiting there
for me.

She says she's **optimistic**
that I'll learn to swim
this year.
I hope so –
kick - kick –
guess we'll wait and see!

PROUD

by Lisa Varchol Perron

I'm proud of my home.
I helped paint the walls!
I'm proud of my drawings
that hang in the halls.

I'm proud of our garden
and yard with a slide.
But mostly I'm proud
of the people inside.

QUEASY

by Katey Howes

I'm riding in the way-back seat.
The road is swervy curvy!
It's fun at first, but then my tum
starts feeling topsy turvy.
Open up the window, please,
and take the next turn easy,
unless you want to see my lunch –
I'm getting very queasy!

RESTLESS

by Elizabeth Kuelbs

When
   I am restless
      energy fizzes
         through me and I
           go all noodley,
              antsy, backbendy,
           prancy, floppy,
         fidgety, hoppy,
      dancy . . . until
   I am calm
again.

SCARED

by Rochelle Melander

You bite the bugs that bug the beans.
You catch the pests that pester me.
You snack on ants.
You save the plants.
But you are scared of ME!

TIRED

by Kelly Conroy

Blink, blink.
Stretch, stretch.
Rub my eyes
and *yaawwwnnnn*.

But once I take
a little nap,
my tired will
be gone.

UPSET

by Vicki Wilke

My bike goes lickety split.
I cruise around and round.
But sometimes wheels get wobbly,
and BOOM! I'm on the ground!

At first I feel upset,
and so I count . . . to . . . ten.
Then Daddy sticks a bandage on –
and off I go again!

VICTORIOUS

by Anastasia Suen

Yes,
I can!

Yes,
I did!

Yes,
I am
victorious!

WORRIED

by Naomi Shihab Nye

My head keeps rattling abuzz.
My stomach is filled with fuzz.

Can you hear me jiggling inside?
I close my worried eyes

And try to feel like the sun
Warming the floor of my room.

I breathe in deeply and smile.
The calm comes back in a while.

XENIAL

by Willeena Booker

X marks the spot where we can play

Enter my house, please say you'll stay

No grownups allowed, hip-hip-hooray!

I am here to welcome you in

A game of pretend will make us grin

Laughing together, let the fun begin!

YUCKY

by Marty Lapointe-Malchik

My nose keeps running.
Cough keeps coming.
No matter what I do.
We'd better stay apart today
or you'll feel yucky, too.

ZANY

by Marcie Flinchum Atkins

We slip on our wings.
We zip through the grass.
Two zany heroes on guard!

We jump to the sun.
We thump in bare feet.
We fly in our backyard!

A B C D E F G

H I J K

L M N O P

Q R S T U V

W X Y Z

ALPHABET CHOICES

by Janet Wong

Today's a big day for me.
My teacher can tell
I'm feeling strange.

She asks if I'm:
    (a) nervous
    (b) excited
    (c) restless
or
    (d) queasy

How do you feel?

That's easy:
    (e) all of the above!

RESOURCES FOR PARENTS & TEACHERS

TIPS FOR READERS

Here are some basic strategies for sharing poetry with children. Whether you're a family member, caregiver, teacher, librarian, or school administrator, these tips will help you get kids excited about reading!

Reading the pictures
With very young children, reading begins with everything EXCEPT the words. Encourage children to "read" or interpret the pictures and talk about what they see. They can even act out the key word like *excited*, *mad*, *scared*, or *tired*. Movement and play are an important part of learning too.

Reading aloud
Even if your child can read independently, it's good to hear poems read aloud for their sound qualities. Poems are meant to be read out loud to savor the words, sounds, and rhythm. Plus, reading aloud together is a bonding time that makes reading a positive experience for young children just beginning to master the skills of reading.

Props and pantomime
Whether you're reading to a group of children or just one child, simple props or pantomime can make your read-aloud come alive. Use a common object mentioned in the poem as a "poetry prop" and hold it up while reading aloud, such as a pair of scissors while reading *Nervous* or crayons while reading *Proud*. Or use gestures like rubbing your eyes when reading the poem *Tired*.

Combine listening and reading with echo reading
With echo reading, a child or a group of children will repeat lines of a poem after hearing you read them. Pause after each line and put a hand to your ear to cue your readers to repeat what they've just heard.

Point to words
Pointing to words as you read them is a great way to help children learn to read and helps them begin to associate the spoken word with the written word. It also reinforces the concept that English text moves from left to right, top to bottom.

Encourage guessing
Children often like rhyming poems because it's easy to guess the words that come at regular rhyming intervals. They sometimes will guess the wrong words, but it's good to encourage guessing; it makes reading feel like a game and builds prediction skills essential to comprehension.

Read parts
Some poems have a repeated word or phrase that you can point out before you start reading. You can read just the line with those repeated words before you read the whole poem. Children can join in when they hear those repeated words or phrases.

Read, respond, and be open
Talking about our feelings is an important part of processing those feelings and poems can help us do that. As you read these poems aloud, be open to children's responses; they often notice surprising things and make interesting connections. It's also fine just to read a poem and move on.

Record the reading
Record a poem to share with a friend or family member far away. It's easy to make an audio or video recording of a child reading either alone or together with you; simply use your phone or an online tool like Zoom or Google Meet. Or record yourself reading for your child to enjoy later when you may be away.

FUN ACTIVITIES TO TRY

Here are some activities for having fun with poetry in more creative ways after you've read and shared each poem.

Poem titles
Each poem has a one-word title and that word also appears in the poem itself in a different color. This makes it easy for children to join in on that key word as you read the rest of the poem aloud and point to the word when it's their turn.

Learning letters
After reading the poem aloud, challenge children to think of other words that start with the same initial letter. For example, for A = AMAZED, you might offer *apple, alligator, art*, etc. For B = BRAVE, you might offer *ball, bear, boat, banana*, and so on.

Feelings
Every poem in this book focuses on emotion or "feelings" words: *amazed, brave, curious, determined, excited, frustrated, grateful, happy, inspired, jealous, kooky, lonely, mad, nervous, optimistic, proud, queasy, restless, scared, tired, upset, victorious, worried, xenial, yucky,* and *zany*. Brainstorm more feelings words with children and talk about when we might experience those feelings.

Time for poetry
Reading a poem out loud takes less than a minute! Add a quick poem to your routine to build incidental literacy development. Start the day with a poem at breakfast, copy and add a poem to a lunch bag, or end the day with a poem read at dinner or at bedtime. Commemorate the first day of school with a poem, or the last day of school, or "moving up" day. You can also share a poem to celebrate a birthday.

Translate
Translate your favorite poem into another language spoken in your family or community. You can work with a friend or a neighbor or try GoogleTranslate to see how your poem sounds in French or Chinese or another language.

Poems in parts
Several poems in this book use italics, quotation marks, or all capital letters for key words or phrases. As you read aloud, cue children to read the word or phrase in italics, quotes, or capitals in *Curious, Frustrated, Jealous, Kooky, Mad, Nervous, Optimistic, Tired,* or *Upset.*

Body parts and movement
Many of the poems in this book refer to body parts and movement within the poem, such as in *Amazed, Brave, Determined, Optimistic, Restless,* and *Zany.* Invite children to point to each body part as you read the poem out loud or act out the motions described in the poem.

Family poems
Several poems are about moments we share with our families. Work with children to share *Grateful* or *Proud* with their families, *Inspired, Lonely* or *Upset* with parents and caregivers, and *Frustrated* or *Jealous* with siblings.

Types of poems
There are several different types of poems in this book, some rhyming like *Happy* and some free verse or non-rhyming like *Brave* or *Curious.* One poem even has an acrostic built in (see the vertical letters that spell XENIAL in *Xenial*). Challenge children to use their names (or other words) to write their own acrostic poem.

WEB RESOURCES

There are so many useful literacy resources online that it's sometimes hard to know where to start. You'll find basic information and engaging activities at the following recommended websites. Dive in and have fun!

childmind.org
The Child Mind Institute is a research-based resource for families and caregivers on mental health and brain development. Accessible in both English and Spanish.

colorincolorado.org
Colorín Colorado is a national multimedia project that offers bilingual activities and advice for educators and families of English language learners (ELLs).

everychildareader.net
Every Child a Reader connects book creators with learning communities, providing literacy tools and resources. Their many outreach programs include the Kids' Book Choice Awards.

healthiergeneration.org
Alliance for a Healthier Generation works with schools, youth organizations, and businesses to support children's physical and social-emotional health.

ibby.org
The International Board on Books for Young People (IBBY) is an international network with dozens of chapters all over the world working together to connect children with books.

mhanational.org/what-every-child-needs-good-mental-health
Mental Health America has a variety of excellent online resources for understanding and developing children's mental and emotional needs.

naeyc.org
The National Association for the Education of Young Children (NAEYC) is a membership organization that provides professional development and support for early childhood educators and families.

pbs.org/parents/learn-grow/all-ages/emotions-self-awareness
PBS offers parents guidance on developing young children's self-awareness and emotional health, including information on ages and stages, games, crafts, articles, and suitable programs.

raisingchildren.net.au
This parenting website from Australia is full of helpful information and videos including understanding and managing emotions with young children.

reachoutandread.org
Endorsed by the American Academy of Pediatrics (AAP), this site provides early literacy tools in Spanish, screen-free activities, and links to even more resources for reading with children.

usbby.org
The United States Board on Books for Young People (USBBY) is the U.S. national section of IBBY, with an Outstanding International Books List that features titles for children that promote global understanding.

ABOUT THE POETS

You probably found some favorite poems when reading this book. Write down the poets' names and learn more about them by visiting their websites and blogs. Then look for more of their poems (and books)!

Marcie Flinchum Atkins   marcieatkins.com
Marcie Flinchum Atkins is a school librarian and the author of several nonfiction books including *Wait, Rest, Pause: Dormancy in Nature*. She loves to play with zany words to create poems.

Carmen T. Bernier-Grand   carmentberniergrand.com
Carmen T. Bernier-Grand is an award-winning author of twelve books for children and young adults. Her latest book is *We Laugh Alike/Juntos nos reímos*. Frustrated that she is shrinking, she says the "T" in her name stands for "Tall."

Willeena Booker   Twitter: @WilleenaB
Willeena Booker is a poet whose work was published by Moonstone Arts Center and Poetry X Hunger. Her poem "One Voice" was arranged by world-renowned composer Rollo Dilworth with the support of HHEF and the HHHS chorus '22. She loves being xenial in her classroom.

Rose Cappelli   imaginethepossibilitiesblog.wordpress.com
Rose Cappelli spent many years teaching children how to read. Now she writes picture books and poems for them. She still gets a little nervous when speaking in front of an audience.

Kelly Conroy   kellyconroy.com
Kelly Conroy is a children's book writer, poet, and former actuary who loves all things magical, whimsical, and numerical. Her goal in life is to make people smile. Because she is frequently tired, one of her favorite things to do is sleep.

Karen Elise Finch   Twitter: @nestofbooks
Karen Elise Finch has shared her love of words and images as a preschool teacher, art educator, library assistant, and reading tutor. She is very excited to be a contributing poet in *Things We Feel*.

Douglas Florian   douglasflorian.com
Douglas Florian is an artist and author of many acclaimed picture book poetry collections he has both written and illustrated, like ZOOBILATIONS! He is often inspired by the natural world and loves to do research before writing his poems.

Patricia J. Franz   patriciajfranz.com
Patricia J. Franz writes picture books and poetry. She is most jealous of happy dogs, bubbly children, and joyful grandparents, so she tries to emulate them.

Katey Howes   kateyhowes.com
Katey Howes writes poetry and prose for children and adults. She gets a little queasy when she imagines running out of bookshelves, ice cream, or craft supplies.

Carol-Ann Hoyte   poetryinvoice.com/poems/poets/carol-ann-hoyte
Carol-Ann Hoyte is a poet in Montreal, Quebec. She loves novels in verse and serves on the board of Canada's Poetry in Voice. She was mighty brave when she worked as a librarian in an all-boys school for nearly 15 years.

Michelle Kogan   michellekogan.com
Michelle Kogan is a poet, writer, and artist. Her most recent publication appears in the anthology *Imperfect: Poems about Mistakes, Volume II*. Her love of nature and humanity inspire her creative juices and keep her continuously curious.

Marty Lapointe-Malchik   imarty.com
Marty Lapointe-Malchik is a poet and collage artist who also works with families of children who are deaf and hard of hearing. She thinks feeling yucky has its perks, especially when a book of poetry is handy.

Elizabeth Kuelbs   elizabethkuelbs.com
Elizabeth Kuelbs is a writer and poet whose work appears in many publications for children and adults. Her favorite way to calm restless energy is hiking the sunny mountain trails near her home.

Carmela A. Martino   carmelamartino.com
Carmela A. Martino is the author of two novels as well as poems and short stories published in numerous anthologies. Gazing out her kitchen window while doing dishes, she is often amazed by the variety of animals that visit her small backyard.

Juli Mayer   Twitter: @JuliMayer2644
Juli Mayer's poems have appeared in magazines and anthologies such as *Hop to It: Poems to Get You Moving*. She's grateful for babysitting her first granddaughter, who warms her heart.

Rochelle Melander   rochellemelander.com
Rochelle Melander is the author of *Mightier Than the Sword: Rebels, Reformers, and Revolutionaries Who Changed the World through Writing*. When she gets scared, she holds onto a stuffed turtle and the stories of brave explorers.

Naomi Shihab Nye   poetryfoundation.org/poets/naomi-shihab-nye
Naomi Shihab Nye was the Young People's Poet Laureate 2019-2022 and is the author and editor of many award-winning poetry collections. Some days she is worried about all the things we throw away and likes to pick up trash on her neighborhood walks.

Lisa Varchol Perron   lisaperronbooks.com
Lisa Varchol Perron is a children's poet and author. Her debut picture book, *Patterns Everywhere* (Lerner/Millbrook), will be released in 2023. She is proud to share her writing with kids, including her own book-loving daughters.

Joyce Schriebman   joyceschriebman.com
Joyce Schriebman is a writer, rhymer, and social justice striver. She runs an interfaith nonprofit, and her kooky picture book, *Oy Santa!*, will be published in 2024.

Anastasia Suen   asuen.com
Anastasia Suen is the author (and ghostwriter) of more than 400 books for children, teens, and adults. She feels victorious when persistence pays off and "Yes, I can" changes to "Yes, I did" at last.

Pamela Taylor   pamelabtaylor.com
Pamela Taylor writes children's books and poetry. Her debut picture book, *Remy, The Mullet with a Mullet* is forthcoming. She is bound and determined to promote poetry for young children.

Linda J. Thomas   lindajthomas.com
Linda J. Thomas's poems have appeared in anthologies such as the *10.10 Poetry Anthology*. She lives with her husband and the many birds, rabbits, and deer that visit her gardens, so she is hardly ever lonely.

Fernanda Valentino   Twitter: @fgvalentino
Fernanda Valentino was born and raised in Perth, Australia, and now lives in Chicago. Her poems have appeared in *Highlights Hello!* and *High Five Magazine*. She has also translated books from French to English. Traveling and experiencing other cultures makes her happy.

Vicki Wilke   winningwriters.com/people/vicki-wilke
Vicki Wilke taught young children for 33 years while joyfully writing and publishing poetry for adults and her students. She loves writing for and being with her five grandchildren and gets upset when it has been too long!

Matthew Winter   Twitter: @Baileysdad420
Matthew Winter is a teacher. This is his first published work. He loves writing and spending time with his poodle-son, Bailey. When he gets mad, a hug from Bailey makes everything better.

POEM CREDITS

These poems are used with the permission of the author, with all rights reserved. To request reprint rights, please send an email to info@pomelobooks.com and we'll connect you with the poets.

Marcie Flinchum Atkins: "ZANY"; © 2022 by Marcie Flinchum Atkins.

Carmen T. Bernier-Grand: "FRUSTRATED"; © 2022 by Carmen T. Bernier-Grand.

Willeena Booker: "XENIAL"; © 2022 by Willeena Booker.

Rose Cappelli: "NERVOUS"; © 2022 by Rose Cappelli.

Kelly Conroy: "TIRED"; © 2022 by Kelly Conroy.

Karen Elise Finch: "EXCITED"; © 2022 by Karen Elise Finch.

Douglas Florian: "INSPIRED"; © 2022 by Douglas Florian.

Patricia J. Franz: "JEALOUS"; © 2022 by Patricia J. Franz.

Katey Howes: "QUEASY"; © 2022 by Katey Howes.

Carol-Ann Hoyte: "BRAVE"; © 2022 by Carol-Ann Hoyte.

Michelle Kogan: "CURIOUS"; © 2022 by Michelle Kogan.

Elizabeth Kuelbs: "RESTLESS"; © 2022 by Elizabeth Kuelbs.

Marty Lapointe-Malchik: "YUCKY"; © 2022 by Marty Lapointe-Malchik.

Carmela A. Martino: "AMAZED"; © 2022 by Carmela A. Martino.

Juli Mayer: "GRATEFUL"; © 2022 by Juli Mayer.

Rochelle Melander: "SCARED"; © 2022 by Rochelle Melander.

Naomi Shihab Nye: "WORRIED"; © 2022 by Naomi Shihab Nye.

Lisa Varchol Perron: "PROUD"; © 2022 by Lisa Varchol Perron.

Joyce Schriebman: "KOOKY"; © 2022 by Joyce Schriebman.

Anastasia Suen: "VICTORIOUS"; © 2022 by Anastasia Suen.

Pamela Taylor: "DETERMINED"; © 2022 by Pamela Taylor.

Linda J. Thomas: "LONELY"; © 2022 by Linda J. Thomas.

Fernanda Valentino: "HAPPY"; © 2022 by Fernanda Valentino.

Vicki Wilke: "UPSET"; © 2022 by Vicki Wilke.

Matthew Winter: "MAD"; © 2022 by Matthew Winter.

Janet Wong: "OPTIMISTIC," "ALPHABET CHOICES"; © 2022 by Janet S. Wong.

ABOUT VARDELL & WONG

Sylvia M. Vardell recently retired as Professor in the School of Library and Information Studies at Texas Woman's University where she taught graduate courses in children's and young adult literature for more than 20 years. Vardell has published extensively, including five books on literature for children as well as over 25 book chapters and 100 journal articles. In 2020, she curated the anthology *A World Full of Poems: Inspiring Poetry for Children*. She is so grateful for all the poets she gets to work with – especially her friend Janet Wong. Learn more about Vardell at SylviaVardell.com.

Janet Wong is a graduate of Yale Law School and a former lawyer. She has written more than 35 books for children on a wide variety of subjects, including chess (*Alex and the Wednesday Chess Club*) and yoga (*TWIST: Yoga Poems*). She is the 2021 winner of the NCTE Excellence in Poetry for Children Award, a lifetime achievement award that is one of the highest honors a children's poet can receive. Janet is an optimistic person most of the time, and though she cannot swim very well, she is sure that this could change with a little more practice. Learn more about her at JanetWong.com.

Together, Vardell & Wong are the creative forces behind Pomelo Books.

ABOUT POMELO BOOKS

Pomelo Books is Poetry PLUS. Poetry PLUS play. Poetry PLUS science. Poetry PLUS holidays. Poetry PLUS pets – and more. We make it EASY to share poetry any time of day!

Successful K-12 teachers and administrators build regular "touch points" into their routines to create a safe and engaging learning environment. Poetry can be a powerful tool for offering a shared literary experience in just a few minutes, with both curricular benefits and emotional connections for students at all levels.

Our books in The Poetry Friday Anthology series and the Poetry Friday Power Book series make it easy to use poetry for integrating skills, building language learning, crossing curricular areas, mentoring young writers, promoting critical thinking, fostering social-emotional development, and inviting students to respond creatively.

A shared poetry moment can help build a classroom community filled with kindness, respect, and joy. Learn more at PomeloBooks.com.

OTHER BOOKS BY
VARDELL & WONG

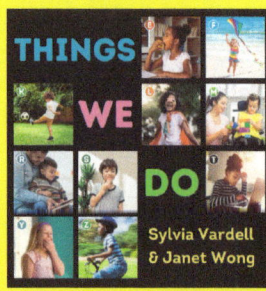

Things We Do
A CBC Hot Off the Press selection

What things do we love to do? In this book you'll find poems from A to Z, featuring action words and photos that will make kids eager to ASK, BEND, CLAP, DANCE, EAT, FLY, GROW, HUG, INVENT, JUMP, KICK, LAUGH, MAKE, NAP, OPEN, PLAY, QUACK, READ, SIGN, TYPE, UNPACK, VISIT, WAVE, X-RAY, YAWN, and ZOOM as you read the playful poems.

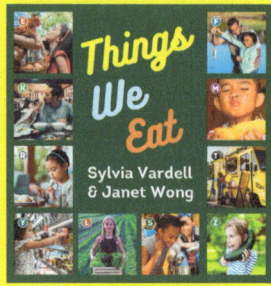

Things We Eat
A POETS.org Summer Books List for Young Readers selection

What things do we love to eat? AVOCADO, BAGEL, COOKIE, DUMPLING, EGG, FISH, GRAPE, HAMBURGER, ICING, JAM, KIMCHI, LETTUCE, MANGO, and lots more!

100% of the profits from this "THINGS WE . . . " series will be donated to the IBBY Children in Crisis Fund (IBBY.org).

Hop to It: Poems to Get You Moving
A Kids' Book Choice Award "Best Book of Facts" Winner

This anthology of 100 poems by 90 poets gets kids thinking and moving as they use pantomime, sign language, and whole body movements, including deskercise! You'll also find poems on current topics, such as life during a pandemic. Take a 30-second indoor recess whenever you need it!

The Poetry Friday Anthology for Celebrations

ILA Notable Books for a Global Society

This fun book features 156 poems (in both Spanish & English) honoring a wide variety of traditional and non-traditional holidays from all over the world. Also available in a Teacher/Librarian Edition.

"A bubbly and educational bilingual poetry anthology for children." – Kirkus

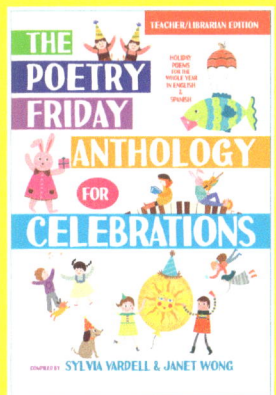

Pet Crazy: A Poetry Friday Power Book

A CBC Hot Off the Press selection

This interactive story – with Hidden Language Skills that engage kids in "playing" with punctuation, spelling, and other basics – features three characters who love spending time with animals. Extensive back matter features resources for helping young people perform, read, write, and try to publish poetry.

"An enthusiastic invitation for kids to celebrate their animal friends through poetry composition." – Kirkus

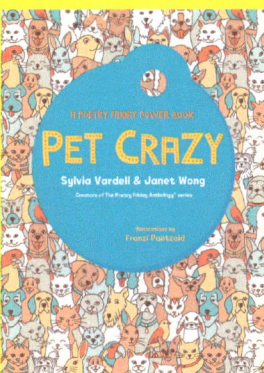

The Poetry of Science

An NSTA Recommends selection

The Poetry of Science is an illustrated book for children that contains 250 poems on science, technology, engineering, and math organized by topic. A companion Teacher/Librarian Edition features mini-lessons and resources.

"A treasury of the greatest science poetry for children ever written, with a twist." – NSTA

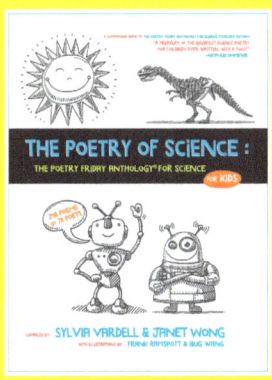

www.ingramcontent.com/pod-product-compliance
Lightning Source LLC
Chambersburg PA
CBHW042048120526
44592CB00030B/24